PRAYERS FOR DIVORCED CATHOLICS

Monica Frese

This work is dedicated to:

The Holy Spirit, who ignites in my heart a deep love
for those suffering through separation/divorce
My husband, who inspires my work and
demonstrates God's endless love for me
My parents, who gave me the greatest gift: my
Catholic Faith
Leslie, whose inner strength through chronic trials
reveals the goodness and dignity of life

TABLE OF CONTENTS

INTRODUCTION

The Blessed Mother told St. Faustina,"Be courageous. Do not fear apparent obstacles, but fix your gaze upon the Passion of my Son, and in this way, you will be victorious." I believe this to be true because I have experienced it.

In the autumn of 2004 I was a single parent of three young children in the midst of a contentious divorce. I had no frame of reference for divorce, the only one in my family of nine children having experienced it. I also had no local family support. I did, however, have that "pearl of great price," my Catholic Faith.

Each day before preschool pick up, I would slip into the empty church for a few minutes of peace. This is when the treasure of *The Stations of the Cross* was exposed to me. The truth was that the deep pain I was experiencing made no sense at all, except in light of the suffering endured by Christ in His Passion. So, as I sought to understand my own grief, Jesus revealed Himself to me. I saw Him rejected, betrayed, mocked, humiliated, harshly judged. Truly, He did understand the pain and contempt I was experiencing. He became my dearest friend. This is when my healing began.

May you come to know the profound, personal love that Jesus and Mary have for you as you pray these meditations. And may the suffering you experience as you seek God's will as a divorced Catholic be the very means to a deep, lasting conversion of heart. May God renew and restore you, and grant you His precious gift of hope.

"Suffering, pain, sorrow, humiliation, feelings of loneliness, are nothing but the kiss of Jesus, a sign that you have come so close that he can kiss you." St. Mother Teresa of Calcutta

In Christ,

Monica Frese
August 27, 2015
The Feast of Saint Monica

CHAPTER ONE

The Rosary

HOW TO PRAY THE ROSARY[1]

1. Make the Sign of the Cross.

2. Holding the Crucifix, say the Apostles' Creed.

3. On the first bead, say an Our Father.

4. Say three Hail Marys on each of the next three beads.

5. Say the Glory Be

6. For each of the five decades, announce and read the Mystery, then say the Our Father.

While fingering each of the ten beads of the decade, next say ten Hail Marys while meditating on the Mystery.

Then say a Glory Be.

After finishing each decade, some say the following prayer requested by the Blessed Virgin Mary at Fatima:

"O my Jesus, forgive us our sins, save us from the fires of hell,lead all souls to Heaven, especially those who have most need of your mercy."

After saying the five decades, say the Hail, Holy Queen:

Hail, holy Queen, mother of mercy, our life, our sweetness, and our hope. To thee do we cry, poor banished children of Eve. To thee do we send up our sighs mourning and weeping in this valley of tears. Turn then, most gracious advocate, thine eyes of mercy toward us, and after this our exile show us the blessed fruit of thy womb, Jesus. O clement, O loving, O sweet Virgin Mary.

(Verse) Pray for us, O Holy Mother of God.

(Response) That we may be made worthy of the promises of Christ.

Next say the Rosary Prayer:

Verse: Let us pray,

Response: O God, whose only begotten Son, by His life, death, and resurrection, has purchased for us the rewards of eternal salvation. Grant, we beseech Thee, that while meditating on these mysteries of the most holy Rosary of the Blessed Virgin Mary, that we may both imitate what they contain and obtain what they promise, through Christ our Lord. Amen.

Most Sacred Heart of Jesus, have mercy on us.

Immaculate Heart of Mary, pray for us.

Followed by this dialogue and prayer:

Verse: Pray for us, O holy Mother of God.

Response: That we may be made worthy of

the promises of Christ.

Let us pray: O God, whose Only Begotten Son,
by his life, Death, and Resurrection,
has purchased for us the rewards of eternal life,
grant, we beseech thee,
that while meditating on these mysteries
of the most holy Rosary of the Blessed Virgin Mary,
we may imitate what they contain
and obtain what they promise,
through the same Christ our Lord. Amen.

The Joyful Mysteries

THE FIRST JOYFUL MYSTERY
THE ANNUNCIATION

Oh, Most Blessed Mother and my Mother, through this mystery, I ask for your motherly intersession. I know the angel and his unexpected news frightened you. This abrupt change in plans for your life must have caused you great confusion and concern about your future.

Well, I am frightened too. The unexpected news of my divorce has disrupted the plans I had for my future. I am so worried for myself and for my children. I need the grace to put this all in God's most capable hands. I realize that this will require so much trust. Help me, Mother, to be steeped in the reality that God has a plan for my life; that He is with me every step of the way. I ask for the grace to replace my fear with trust. Amen.

Our Father - 10 Hail Marys - Glory Be - Fatima Prayer

THE SECOND JOYFUL MYSTERY
THE VISITATION

Oh, Most Blessed Mother and my Mother, through this mystery, I ask for your motherly intersession. Although you were pondering the deep mystery of the Incarnation and trying to make sense of the new reality that you were facing, you stirred the love in your heart to turn the focus off of yourself and to reach out in service to your cousin Elizabeth.

Sometimes I feel as though I can't stop thinking about the divorce, the constant battles, and our uncertain future. I have been consumed with my problems and have made no time for others in my life who deserve my time and attention. Please grant me the grace of humility. Help me to dwell on myself less and on others more. Amen.

Our Father - 10 Hail Marys - Glory Be - Fatima Prayer

THE THIRD JOYFUL MYSTERY
THE NATIVITY

Oh Most Blessed Mother and my Mother, through
this mystery, I ask for your motherly intercession.
I'm sure that you had taken great care to prepare
your home with Joseph for the arrival of your
baby. Plans changed again when required to travel
to Bethlehem for the census. It's hard to imagine
the conditions that you and St. Joseph endured as
you welcomed Jesus, Our Savior, into the world.
You had no material means to provide for your
baby. You had nowhere to stay. You lived in total
poverty and yet all accounts tell us that your heart
was filled with joy! You were disinterested in the
material things of this world because you had the
better part – Jesus, Himself.

Please grant me the grace to be detached from
inconsequential material things that I cling to so
tightly. Placing such value in possessions is

causing me to lose my peace. Litigation could cause me to lose them all. What my heart really desires is peace. I need the grace to remain close to Jesus, who will always be the true source of my security and my joy. Amen

Our Father - 10 Hail Marys - Glory Be - Fatima Prayer

THE FOURTH JOYFUL MYSTERY
THE PRESENTATION

Oh, Most Blessed Mother and my Mother, through this mystery, I ask for your motherly intercession. I am so amazed as I reflect on the obedience with which you and Joseph lived your humble lives. You knew that yours was a virgin birth and did not require the purification of this temple visit. You knew that your son was the Savior that the world had been anticipating. Yet, you humbly honored the teachings and requirements of your faith set out before you.

As I carry this cross of divorce, please grant me the grace to be obedient to the Church's teachings. There are many things I don't understand. I feel as though I don't fit in anymore and that I've been hurt. Therefore, I'd like to exempt myself from certain teachings. Please help me to seek true understanding, not just form ideas and opinions. I do want to be obedient like you, Mary, but it's so hard. I know that I want to live in the Truth and that God will reveal His will to me as long as I humble myself , pray, and obey. Amen.

Our Father - 10 Hail Marys - Glory Be - Fatima Prayer

THE FIFTH JOYFUL MYSTERY
THE FINDING OF JESUS IN THE TEMPLE

Oh, Most Blessed Mother and my Mother, through this mystery, I ask for your motherly intercession. I can imagine the urgency with which you and St. Joseph must have searched for Jesus when he was missing for three days. Pursuing your son, whom you both loved so much was surely your singular focus. The relief and joy you experienced upon finding Jesus must have been tangible!

I'm so afraid that I may become lost. My life has become so chaotic and I don't even recognize my old life anymore. I don't want to get lost from my family, friends or my Catholic Faith, but the world is pulling me in so many directions! Please hear my plea, Mary; that you will always search for me, seek me, pursue me with the same sense of urgency that you searched for Jesus when he was lost. Better yet, send your Spouse, The Holy Spirit, to direct my course of action so that I don't get lost at all! Amen.

Our Father - 10 Hail Marys - Glory Be - Fatima Prayer

The Sorrowful Mysteries

THE FIRST SORROWFUL MYSTERY
THE AGONY IN THE GARDEN

Oh, Most Blessed Mother and my Mother, through this mystery, I ask for your motherly intercession. As I meditate on your son's agony in the garden, I am struck by the depth of his sorrow. My heart is so heavy when I think of him looking for the support of his friends and finding them asleep. How could they sleep at a time like this?

I often feel alone in my suffering too. How could my spouse have abandoned me? Where are the people in my life who were so anxious to be with me when things were happy? Today I unite my suffering with Jesus. I pray for the same grace and comfort that Jesus received from the angel in the garden during his Agony. Be the source of my strength Jesus, that in you I will have strength for everything. Amen.

Our Father - 10 Hail Marys - Glory Be - Fatima Prayer

THE SECOND SORROWFUL MYSTERY
THE SCOURGING AT THE PILLAR

Oh, Most Blessed Mother and my Mother, through this mystery, I ask for your motherly intercession. As I meditate on your son's horrific scourging, I am struck by the hatred and violence of the soldiers, who inflicted such devastating, unjust punishment. I have experienced the deep wounds that hatred and vengeance have inflicted in my heart. Today I unite my suffering with Jesus. As I endure the pain inflicted on me through my divorce, I pray for the grace to be charitable, especially to the one who has hurt me the most. Let me never trade evil for evil. Please heal those wounds that are still causing my heart so much pain. Be the source of my strength Jesus, that in you I will have strength for everything. Amen.

Our Father - 10 Hail Marys - Glory Be - Fatima Prayer

THE THIRD SORROWFUL MYSTERY
THE CROWNING WITH THORNS

Oh, Most Blessed Mother and my Mother, through this mystery, I ask for your motherly intercession. As I meditate on your son's crowning with thorns, I am scandalized by the level of mockery and humiliation that Jesus had to endure. He was made to look like a fool.

The circumstances surrounding my divorce are humiliating to me, too. Personal stories have been circulating publicly and people have been left to speculate about our family. I feel exposed and mocked. Today I unite my suffering with Jesus. As I carry my cross of divorce, I pray for the grace of humility, especially when I want to explain it all away. Give me the confidence to trust that you know the truth. Be the source of my strength Jesus, that in you I will have strength for everything. Amen.

Our Father - 10 Hail Marys - Glory Be - Fatima Prayer

THE FOURTH SORROWFUL MYSTERY
THE CARRYING OF THE CROSS

Oh, Most Blessed Mother and my Mother, through this mystery, I ask for your motherly intercession. As I meditate on your son as he carried his heavy cross, I am inspired by his fortitude. Although he was beaten, bleeding, and physically exhausted, he persevered out of love for me. My suffering is weighing on me to the point of exhaustion too. At times I feel as though I can't bear it. It often becomes too much for me and I fall beneath the weight of the pain. Today I unite my suffering with Jesus. As I carry my cross of divorce, I pray for the grace of perseverance. When I fall, help me to trust in your mercy and get back up again. Be the source of my strength Jesus, that in you I will have strength for everything. Amen.

Our Father - 10 Hail Marys - Glory Be - Fatima Prayer

THE FIFTH SORROWFUL MYSTERY
THE CRUCIFIXION

Oh, Most Blessed Mother and my Mother, through this mystery I ask for your motherly intercession. As I meditate on the crucifixion and death of your son, I am struck by the reality of the price he paid for my redemption. Jesus had to die in order open the gates of heaven for me, to give me hope for a new, everlasting life with Him. My marriage has been sacrificed too. The plans that I had for my life have died. Today, I unite my suffering with Christ crucified. As I carry my cross of divorce, I pray for the grace of hope. Never let me fall into despair. Help me to surrender my old life and be open to the peace and confidence of a new life lived with Jesus. Be the source of my strength Jesus, that in you I will have strength for everything. Amen.

Our Father - 10 Hail Marys - Glory Be - Fatima Prayer

The Glorious Mysteries

THE FIRST GLORIOUS MYSTERY
THE RESURRECTION

Oh, Most Blessed Mother and my Mother, through this mystery, I ask for your motherly intercession. As I meditate on this mystery, I can imagine Mary Magdalene rushing to the tomb, her heart full of sorrow and pain. She did not expect God to transform her anguish and despair by the joy of Christ's greatest miracle — his resurrection. In the midst of the chaos of my divorce, I am weighted down with sorrow and pain too. As soon as I get through one challenge, different problems appear to take its place. In my moments of discouragement, please grant me the grace of hope. Remind me not to succumb to anxiety and fear. May I always leave room in my heart for you to burst through and replace my sorrow with joy. Amen.

Our Father - 10 Hail Marys - Glory Be - Fatima Prayer

THE SECOND GLORIOUS MYSTERY
THE ASCENSION OF CHRIST INTO HEAVEN

Oh, Most Blessed Mother and my Mother, through this mystery I ask for your motherly intercession. In John 14:1-3, Jesus tells us not to let our hearts be troubled. We learn that he has gone to heaven to prepare a place for us and that he will return to bring us to back to be with him forever. Sometimes I worry that my circumstances, faults, failures and regrets will keep me from realizing this promise. Please teach me about Mercy and Trust. Jesus, I know you will not abandon me. You have also prepared the very graces I need for every circumstance, fault, failure and regret that plague me. The graces, earned for me through your passion and death, are the very building blocks of my place in heaven. Please remind me of this truth when I try to carry my burdens alone, when I stumble and fall. Amen.

Our Father - 10 Hail Marys - Glory Be - Fatima Prayer

THE THIRD GLORIOUS MYSTERY
THE DECENT OF THE HOLY SPIRIT

Oh, Most Blessed Mother and my Mother, through this mystery I ask for your motherly intercession. The disciples must have felt so frightened and alone in those days following Christ's Ascension. In hope, they prayed for courage and for direction. In those quiet moments when the reality that my marriage is over sinks in, I feel alone and scared too. Please grant me the grace to persevere in prayer and to await the outpouring of the Holy Spirit into my soul. Through my personal Pentecost, I will be renewed, refreshed, strengthened and advised. The Holy Spirit is with me to grant me the courage to tackle the challenges of life, and go forth fortified with confidence and trust in God. Amen.

Our Father - 10 Hail Marys - Glory Be - Fatima Prayer

THE FOURTH GLORIOUS MYSTERY
THE ASSUMPTION OF MARY

Oh, Most Blessed Mother and my Mother, through this mystery I ask for your motherly intercession. Mary had to wait many years after Jesus died to be with reunited with him in heaven. From our human perspective, this seems like an impossible task. However, the Church teaches us that we are never truly separated from the intimacy of personal contact with Jesus. We have the Eucharist, and so did Mary. Lord, please sustain me on my journey in faith by granting me the deep desire to receive you frequently in Holy Communion. Mary, please give me the grace to imitate you and your devotion to your son Jesus Christ in the Eucharist. Through the Eucharist, may my broken heart be transformed by the love of Christ. Amen.

Our Father - 10 Hail Marys - Glory Be - Fatima Prayer

THE FIFTH GLORIOUS MYSTERY
THE CROWNING OF MARY QUEEN OF HEAVEN

Oh, Most Blessed Mother and my Mother,
through this mystery I ask for your motherly
intercession. I feel so blessed to have Mary as my
heavenly mother. Thank you, Lord, for this
awesome gift, which you gave us from the cross.
Mary, also known as Our Lady of Sorrows, can
see all of my hurt and all of my pain. I know that
as my Mother, she intercedes for my every need.
This gives me so much solace and peace. As I begin
to rebuild my life, please grant me the grace to
turn to Mary in my every need. Amen.

Our Father - 10 Hail Marys - Glory Be - Fatima Prayer

The Luminous Mysteries

THE FIRST LUMINOUS MYSTERY
THE BAPTISM OF JESUS

Oh, Most Blessed Mother and my Mother, through this mystery, I ask for your motherly intercession. Jesus' baptism in the Jordan reminds me of my own baptism. This was the day that I became a part of his family. The Roman Catholic Church has been my home, my extended family for so many years. It hurts me that I now feel as though I don't quite belong. I want to be healed of the lie that I'm a second class Catholic. Today, I ask for the grace of a fresh start. The waters of baptism that Jesus made clean when he submersed himself gave me a grace that will be with me for the rest of my life. I am a new person in Christ. Please help me as I navigate this road and remind me that each new day is an opportunity for a fresh start. Amen.

Our Father - 10 Hail Marys - Glory Be - Fatima Prayer

THE SECOND LUMINOUS MYSTERY
THE WEDDING FEAST AT CANA

Oh, Most Blessed Mother and my Mother,
through this mystery, I ask for your motherly
intercession. Mary, you were more tuned in to the
needs of the bride and groom than they were! You
anticipated their lack of wine and went straight to
your son for the solution. As a good mother, you
don't like to see us ashamed by poor choices or
lack of due diligence. Stone jars were the vessels
that Christ filled with the water, which turned into
the choice wine. You must see that I have an
empty vessel that needs filling too, Mary. Without
your motherly assistance, I may run out of the
things I need to go on. Please go to Jesus for me.
Fill my heart with patience, forgiveness,
gentleness, humility and trust. Don't let it become
a heart of stone, but tender and humble heart, open

enough to be filled with the love of your Son, Jesus. Amen.

Our Father - 10 Hail Marys - Glory Be - Fatima Prayer

THE THIRD LUMINOUS MYSTERY

Oh, Most Blessed Mother and my Mother, through this mystery, I ask for your motherly intercession. When Jesus began his public ministry and opened the meaning of scripture to the people he encountered it changed their lives. I know that Jesus wants to speak to me through his living word, but sometimes I find it so hard to understand. If the meaning is unclear or doesn't resonate with me, I get discouraged and give up trying. I'm tired of quitting. The world so easily gives up when things require patience, understanding and perseverance. Rampant divorce is a great example of this attitude. Therefore, I beg for the grace of perseverance. We've been taught that if we seek, we will find; if we knock, the door will be opened. So in confidence I commit to continue to seek God's will through prayer and Holy Scripture. Please Mary,

send the Holy Spirit to me as I search for solace
and direction through The Word of God. Amen.

Our Father - 10 Hail Marys - Glory Be - Fatima Prayer

THE FOURTH LUMINOUS MYSTERY
THE TRANSFIGURATION

Oh, Most Blessed Mother and my Mother, through this mystery, I ask for your motherly intercession. James and John climbed up the mountain with Jesus just as they had done many times before. They had seen him perform many miracles throughout the years of their friendship, but Jesus wanted to cement their faith by allowing them to witness his divinity through the Transfiguration. What they believed would be an ordinary day became a holy and divine event. Jesus, I need to know that you are truly present in the circumstances that are unfolding in my life through my divorce. Thank you for the times that you have used the people and events in my life to show me your love and your presence. Please grant me the grace of wonder and hope; that I may always seek to look at my life with the expectancy that you will enter my circumstances as my Divine

Savior, the Son of God. Amen.

Our Father - 10 Hail Marys - Glory Be - Fatima Prayer

THE FIFTH LUMINOUS MYSTERY
THE INSTITUTION OF THE EUCHARIST

Oh, Most Blessed Mother and my Mother, through this mystery, I ask for your motherly intercession. On the night of the Last Supper, your son said, "This is my body given up for you." He has never gone back on that promise. Our Lord knew that I would feel alone and abandoned. He saw that I would need him fully present to me in the Eucharist to strengthen me, to remind me of what true love is. Please grant me the grace to be thankful for the gift of Jesus' true presence in the Eucharist. Help me to desire to show him my love and fidelity by taking more frequent opportunities to receive him at Mass and visit him in Eucharistic Adoration. Amen.

Our Father - 10 Hail Marys - Glory Be - Fatima Prayer

CHAPTER TWO

The Stations of the Cross

Begin with the Sign of the Cross: In the name of the Father, and of the Son, and of the Holy Spirit. Amen.

Opening Scripture Reading

The Son of Man is destined to suffer grievously, to be rejected, and to be raised up on the third day. If anyone wants to be a follower of mine, let him renounce himself and take up his cross every day and follow me. For anyone who wants to save his life will lose it; but anyone who loses his life for my sake, that man will save it (Luke 9:22-24).

Opening Prayer

Lord Jesus, help me to be open to your closeness and presence as I begin this journey to Calvary with you. Help me to find in your Passion and Death the strength to take up my cross and follow you.

FIRST STATION

I adore you, O Christ, and I praise you, because by your holy cross you have redeemed the world.

<u>Meditation</u>: Lord Jesus, often I feel unjustly judged by the court system, just as you were. At times even my friends and family voice their judgmental interpretation of my situation and fail to be understanding or loving. Help me to react as you did, with the quiet confidence of knowing that God our Father knows the truth. Help me to seek you as my most ardent Defender.

Be the source of my strength, that in you I will have strength for everything.

SECOND STATION
JESUS ACCEPTS HIS CROSS

I adore you, O Christ, and I praise you, because by your holy cross you have redeemed the world.

Meditation: Lord Jesus, the cross that you willingly accepted was weighted down by our sins, for you are blameless and without sin. My cross is heavy too, Lord. My sins make it difficult to carry, but the weight placed on it by the person who hurt me most makes it seem unbearable to hold. When the weight of the cross of divorce overwhelms me Lord, prompt me to unite my sufferings with yours. Help me to remember the burden that you bore for my sake.

Be the source of my strength, that in you I will have strength for everything.

THIRD STATION

I adore you, O Christ, and I praise you, because by your holy cross you have redeemed the world.

Meditation: Lord Jesus, over the years I have developed sinful patterns of behavior. These sinful choices coupled with my lack of focus and attention on you helped to create an environment void of peace. Through your mercy and grace, I've come to recognize the part I played in the breakup of my marriage. But patterns are hard to change, Lord. Please give me the grace not to fall back into those sinful patterns. And if I do, help me to remember your first fall. And fill me with the courage to get back up and begin again.

Be the source of my strength, that in you I will have strength for everything.

FOURTH STATION

I adore you, O Christ, and I praise you, because by your holy cross you have redeemed the world.

Meditation: Lord Jesus, when you mother Mary's eyes met yours she was overcome by your suffering. Do I take the time to notice the suffering of others? Sometimes I fear that I am so consumed with my own suffering that I pay little or no attention to what others may be feeling. Open my eyes, Jesus to each opportunity that you provide for me to empathize with those around me. Teach me the true meaning of Humility, one of the greatest virtues of your Blessed Mother. Help me to understand that humility does not mean to think less of myself, but to think of myself less.

Be the source of my strength, that in you I will have strength for everything.

FIFTH STATION
SIMON HELPS CARRY THE CROSS

I adore you, O Christ, and I praise you, because by your holy cross you have redeemed the world.

Meditation: Lord, Jesus in your humility you allowed Simon to help you with the burden of your cross. Many people have reached out to me also in an effort to relieve my suffering. Sometimes I find it so difficult to accept their help, Lord. I'd like to think that I can do it all by myself. I can't. Release me from my prideful tendencies. Help me to accept their help as you accepted the help of Simon.

Be the source of my strength, that in you I will have strength for everything.

SIXTH STATION
VERONICA WIPES THE FACE OF JESUS

I adore you, O Christ, and I praise you, because by your holy cross you have redeemed the world.

Meditation: As I meditate on this station it is easy to see Veronica's compassion for you in your time of sorrow. But what is important here is something more subtle and more powerful: even in the midst of your most painful suffering, you left your imprint on Veronica's cloth as well as her heart. Am I so consumed with being politically correct that I'm afraid to share my faith with others? Teach me, dear Lord, to find ways to leave your imprint on the people I meet today in spite of my hardships.

Be the source of my strength, that in you I will have strength for everything.

SEVENTH STATION
JESUS FALLS THE SECOND TIME

I adore you, O Christ, and I praise you, because by your holy cross you have redeemed the world.

Meditation: Placing myself at the scene of your second fall I can see the soldiers and the crowd laughing at your physical weakness. They make jokes at your expense and they enjoy seeing you fail. They call you names and proclaim you a fraud. I'm ashamed, Lord. How many times have I gotten satisfaction over the falls and failings of the one who has hurt me the most? Sometimes I just wait for some hardship to befall that person so I can publicly humiliate them. Heal my heart Lord. Help me not to repay evil for evil but instead teach me to forgive and forget.

Be the source of my strength, that in you I will have strength for everything.

EIGHTH STATION
JESUS SPEAKS TO THE WOMEN

I adore you, O Christ, and I praise you, because by your holy cross you have redeemed the world.

Meditation: This station used to puzzle me, Lord. I could not understand why you would tell these sorrowful women not to weep for you, but to weep for themselves and for their children. Now I see why. You could see, even then, all of the painful suffering that parents and children would go through when families fall apart. You especially had tremendous compassion and sorrow for the children. I'm so sorry Jesus for all of the pain this is causing my children. Surround them with their Guardian Angels and ask your Blessed Mother to wrap them within her loving mantle. Heal their hearts, Lord.

Be the source of my strength, that in you I will have strength for everything.

NINTH STATION
JESUS FALLS THE THIRD TIME

I adore you, O Christ, and I praise you, because by your holy cross you have redeemed the world.

Meditation: Lord, when I contemplate you falling for the third time it's hard to understand how you were able to go on. So many times I feel as though I can't go on. Just when I think that I've hit a stride another obstacle trips me up and I fall . . . again. Help me to see that when I am most vulnerable, when my heart is broken wide open and I think that my situation is hopeless that you desire my SURRENDER. I want to give it all to you, Jesus. Please teach me how. I cannot do this without you, Lord. Piece together my broken heart and spirit with the healing power of your love.

Be the source of my strength, that in you I will have strength for everything.

TENTH STATION

I adore you, O Christ, and I praise you, because by your holy cross you have redeemed the world.

Meditation: Lord Jesus, seeing you so cruelly humiliated as they intentionally stripped you of your garments grieves my heart. I offer up to you the many humiliations that I have suffered as a result of my divorce. Please strip me of all of my past embarrassments that this divorce has caused me. And clothe me with the virtues of your Blessed Mother: faithfulness, obedience, prudence, patience, mercy and purity.

Be the source of my strength, that in you I will have strength for everything.

ELEVENTH STATION
JESUS IS NAILED TO THE CROSS

I adore you, O Christ, and I praise you, because by your holy cross you have redeemed the world.

Meditation: Christ, you lived in the truth and were nailed to a cross because of it. The crowd preferred to live in darkness surrounded by lies and fueled by hatred. I am so tired of living in darkness. I'm tired of all of the lies and hatred that swirl around me as I see my marriage fall apart. I am going to nail every lie to your cross and plead for the grace to live in the truth. I will no longer accept lies and deception in my life. You are the Way, the Truth and the Life, Jesus. Give me the courage that it takes to live an authentic life as you did.

Be the source of my strength, that in you I will have strength for everything.

TWELFTH STATION

I adore you, O Christ, and I praise you, because by your holy cross you have redeemed the world.

Meditation: I give this moment to you, Jesus. Help me to think of nothing other that the fact that you died for ME. How can I turn my back on you now, Lord? So often I have taken the gift of my faith for granted; going to Mass out of obligation and begrudgingly participating in the sacraments. I'm sorry, Jesus. I am reminded of the Roman soldier whose servant you so mercifully healed. From my heart I utter his prayer, "I believe. Help my unbelief." Help me to realize the richness and fullness of my Catholic Faith. Especially inspire me to desire you, who are fully present in the Eucharist.

Be the source of my strength, that in you I will have strength for everything.

THIRTEENTH STATION

I adore you, O Christ, and I praise you, because by your holy cross you have redeemed the world.

Meditation: My heart breaks when I think of your mother's overwhelming loss. Your lifeless body was taken down from the cross and she lovingly held you in her arms. Jesus, I see the failure of my marriage as an overwhelming loss too. Please encourage me to rely on Mary's motherly love. Help me to place my loss into her loving arms. Open my heart to her consolation. Help me rely on her infinite desire to draw me closer to you, her son.

Be the source of my strength, that in you I will have strength for everything.

FOURTEENTH STATION
JESUS IS LAID IN THE TOMB

I adore you, O Christ, and I praise you, because by your holy cross you have redeemed the world.

Meditation: The tomb was such an empty and cold place for the King of Kings and the Lord of Lords to dwell, even in death. I reflect on my soul, where you also desire to dwell. Is it empty and cold too, Lord? In your great mercy and love for us, Jesus, you have provided an opportunity to soften our hearts and make our souls warm and inviting to your presence: the sacrament of Reconciliation. I need your help to overcome my fear and weakness. Fill me with true contrition for my sins and a deep desire to begin again with the grace you pour down on me in this sacrament of love.

Be the source of my strength, that in you I will have strength for everything.

CHAPTER THREE

Prayers to the Saints

PRAYING TO THE SAINTS

One of the greatest treasures of The Church are the Saints in heaven, who stand at the ready to intercede for our every need and to aid in our journey toward heaven.

<u>The Intercession of the Saints</u>: *"Being more closely united to Christ, those who dwell in heaven fix the whole Church more firmly in holiness….They do not cease to intercede with the Father for us, as they proffer the merits which they acquired on earth through the one mediator between God and men, Christ Jesus. ….So by their fraternal concern is our weakness greatly helped."* - Catechism of the Catholic Church #956

IN TIMES OF PERSECUTION

Dear St. Therese,

From the depth of your heart you proclaimed that you want to spend your heaven doing good on earth. Little Flower, relying on this promise, I seek your help during those times when I feel persecuted. For the times when I am treated with disdain, battered with harsh words, falsely accused, and treated with indifference from the one who has hurt me most, I seek the grace to not only endure, but see with new eyes. For it is well known that you endured harsh treatment, accusation, and rejection from some of those you lived with. Their words and actions were like daggers to your sensitive soul, yet, your response to them was always kind, meek, gentle, charitable, and open to reconciliation. This was your "Little Way." Through this offering of your heart, you found a way to love Jesus in a profound and personal way. This Little Way to holiness was your means to becoming one of our greatest saints and Doctor of the Church! Please pray for the grace for me to grow in holiness by responding to insults and persecution as you did. Help me to be kind, respond gently, and resist trading insult for insult.

For he will command his angels concerning you, to guard you in all your ways. Those who love me, I will deliver; I will protect those who know my name. When they call to me I will answer them; I will be with them in trouble, I will rescue them, and honor them. - Psalm 91: 11, 14-15

IN TIMES OF REJECTION
PRAYER TO ST. HELEN

Dear St. Helen,

You are well known as the Saint who gave us one of our greatest, earthly treasures: The True, Holy Cross of Christ. What many people don't know about you is the fact that around the year 289, at a time when divorce was virtually unheard of, your husband of twenty-seven years divorced you for a younger, politically-influential woman. Your faith, however, was so strong that this suffering, the cross of rejection, propelled you to seek a deep intimacy with Jesus. In spite of your grief and humiliation, you were convicted to fulfill the work set out for you of recovering the relics of Christ's Passion, even into your seventies! The pain of rejection that I have experienced by former spouse is threatening to cause me to become bitter and to let spiritual inertia set in. Please intercede for me, that in spite of feeling rejected, I may sense the deep, faithful, fruitful love of Christ. May this love propel me to realize my purpose, fill me with zeal, and fulfill the work set out for me by God. May I come to love my cross, as Jesus did.

It is right and just to entrust oneself wholly to God and to believe absolutely what he says. It would be futile and false to place such faith in a creature. - Catechism of the Catholic Church #150

PREPARE THE WAY
PRAYER TO ST. JOHN THE BAPTIST

Dear St. John the Baptist,

Please go before me into every contentious encounter. Prepare the way for me in my court proceedings and in every awkward meeting with my former spouse. Make straight my path as I seek to know and to follow God's will for me. I invite you to prepare my heart in advance for any major change that may cause me discouragement. I entrust my cause to you, seeking only the Truth and the strength that I need on my journey.

Truly I tell you, among those born of women there has not risen anyone greater than John the Baptist; yet whoever is least in the kingdom of heaven is greater than he. - Matthew 11:11

PROTECTION FOR CHILDREN
PRAYER TO ST. MAXIMILIAN KOLBE

Dear St. Maximilian Kolbe,

While in Auschwitz during the Nazi occupation, you offered to take the place of a family man who was chosen to die in retaliation for an escaped prisoner. This ultimate act of heroic virtue earned you your martyr's crown. Today I pray for the grace to stand in the place of my children, when they get thrown in the middle of my divorce war. Help me to be their shield from the arrows of anger, hurt, and blame that fly between my former spouse and I. Grant me the humility to take the hit, endure the insult, hold my tongue and gently remove them from the line of fire.

Greater love has no one than this, to lay down one's life for one's friends. - John 15:13

PRAYER FOR REST

Dear St. Raphael the Archangel,

Please come to my bedside to protect me from all bad dreams and bad thoughts. I ask for the grace to ruminate on God, His Mercy, and His Goodness not on the hopeless, painful details of my divorce. Help me to sleep calmly and peacefully all night long and to wake well rested in the morning. In spite of my looming troubles, may I be restored and renewed as I begin each new day.

Then Raphael called the two of them privately and said to them, "Bless God and acknowledge Him in the presence of all the living for the good things He has done for you. - Tobit 12: 6

CHAPTER FOUR

Examination of Conscience

EXAMINATION OF CONSCIENCE FOR
DIVORCED CATHOLICS

I am the LORD your God; you shall not have strange Gods before me.

- Anything that chronically distracts my attention away from my friendship with God will rob my soul of its peace. Therefore, I must look honestly at my life and reflect on the things that draw me away form prayer and the Sacraments.
- Have I developed an attitude of self-sufficiency, determined to do everything by my own strength and power, leaving God out of the equation?
- Have I put new relationships before God?

You shall not take the name of the LORD your God in Vain.

- Have I become careless in my speech, using God's name out of habit rather than out of love and respect?

- In anger, have I spoken the name of God or His Son, Jesus?
- Have I sworn by God's name without considering the gravity of such an assertion?

Remember to keep holy the LORD'S day.
- Have I used my separation or divorce as an excuse to avoid my obligation to attend Sunday Mass?
- Have I done all I can to make sure my kids get to Mass, even when it's inconvenient or requires me to be cooperative with my former spouse?
- Have I let myself be influenced by the culture, which permits things as sports, work, or errands to trump going to Mass?
- Do I justify frequently skipping Mass by telling myself that God understands?

Honor your father and your mother
- How have I treated my parents through

my divorce process?

- Have I distanced myself from my parent's love and support out of shame?
- Have I abused my parents' generosity to help me?
- Have I thanked my parents for the many ways in which they show me love and support?
- Have I remained respectful to my former in-laws?

You shall not kill.

- Have I spread stories about my former spouse that damage their reputation, even if they are true?
- Have I harbored hate in my heart in my heart toward my former spouse or wished that something bad would happen to them?

You shall not commit adultery.

- Was I unfaithful to my spouse?
- Have I sought out relationships out of

revenge for being hurt by my former
spouse?

- After my civil divorce, have I pursued
  dating relationships even if I have not
  received a decree of nullity from the
  Church?

You shall not steal.

- Have I been honest with my former spouse
  and the court as they determined
  distribution of our assets?
- In a spirit of revenge, did I insist on a
  settlement that left my former spouse
  without adequate means to support their
  self?

**You shall not bear false witness against your
neighbor.**

- Did I tell the truth in my court
  proceedings?
- Did I falsely swear under oath about the
  circumstances of my divorce?

- Have I embellished events, which made my former spouse look bad before the children or others?
- Have I given myself permission to lie to my former spouse believing that it's none of their business?
- Have I set a good example for my children, choosing to be honest even when it's difficult?

You shall not covet your neighbor's wife.
- Have I imagined other people's spouse to be the "perfect" spouse?
- Am I jealous of other people's relationships?
- Do I permit myself to wallow in self-pity and envy believing that "it should be me?"

You shall not covet your neighbor's goods.
- Do I harbor anger or resentment over the material things my former spouse was awarded by the court?

- Do I think it's not fair when I see other people enjoying material things that I don't have, blaming my former spouse for my misfortune?

---

[1] www.usccb.org/prayer-and-worship/prayers-and-devotions/rosaries/how-to-pray-the-rosary.cfm
www.ewtn.com/Devotionals/prayers/rosary/how_to.htm

52025854R00050

Made in the USA
Columbia, SC
01 March 2019